THE VERGIL WOODS

THE VERGIL WOODS

Poems *by* HENRY BRAUN

NEW YORK   *1 9 6 8*   *Atheneum*

These days appeared first in OUT OF THE WAR SHADOW and is reprinted here by permission of Denise Levertov Goodman and the publisher, War Resisters' League. Others of these poems have previously appeared in AUDIENCE, CHELSEA 9, COLORADO STATE REVIEW, THE MASSACHUSETTS REVIEW, MIDSTREAM, THE NATION, and PRAIRIE SCHOONER.

For Joan

CONTENTS

THE VERGIL WOODS

ADAM NAMING

My body is tired for the birds that have flown from me;
Their fathomless wings are riding from my brow
In echoes. I have finished naming now:
They are not lost that fall by an unmapped sea.

Twilight is home for wrens in the great oak trees
And for the hawk that in grey caves has lain,
The peacock, host of the rainbow after rain,
And river swan, pearl of earth's necklaces.

Nests are arrayed and shingled in the air
Beneath the wandering aegis of a word
Chosen by me. When mating calls are heard
My poem moves in the desiring pair.

Envied by huntsmen I numbered the animals
Gathered from nature in my baptistery;
The unicorn pranced, eyes arched in mystery,
And zebras passed musing on parallels.

I have uplifted tents within my mind
For timeless griffins with vague wings outspread
And serpents of the field. Even the dead
Are sung and not to quietness resigned.

They have all gone like music from my keeping
Towards the named world. Left in this silent garden,
Tired of my duties as its lonely warden,
I seek forgetfulness at last in sleeping.

THE NEW ADAM

"We are wandering encyclopedias" NIETZSCHE

I will bring the lion under my roof,
the fieldmouse and the timidest of hares,
cobras, the griffin—it exists now—the onager,
and wander, dying, through
that terrible zoo.

Then having shed through death my animals,
as the new Adam I'll awake,
survive that death and awake,
the garden as a simple flower before me.

In its wet depth I hope to see my face.

THE SCHOLAR

I am alone with my fish in the fishbowl,
Getting used to fins, unused to fingers.
Through naked stretches of the bowl we swim
Beyond the schools. The noises of school life
Come clinking across the water-colored pale—
I, towards my great fact turning, ignore.

Oh, grey and immense, his scales hang like a wall
Of shutters breathing to the water's lung.
A ray of sunlight flips them into glory.
I swim freestyle, unnoticeably small,
And butt very gently on that flank.

Have I stopped for long? Many hours are lonely.
The wrinkles on my fingers near the bone.
Yet when the light from him pours through my eyes
A rainbow spans my dark interior
And I linger. Some days we browse in quietness, some
Sub specie aeternitatis paddle on.

FOR AN OLD TEACHER

So unhappily magnified to me,
This man, who sees me as small
As I see him large,
Both looking through the same telescope
At different ends.
Others disparage him to me; some tear him down.
A few, perhaps, praise me to him.
But when at rare times we meet
Inescapably on the lonely sidewalk
And cannot talk,
We edge around each other like gamebirds
Of different species.
And because that is so,
The instrument will not come down for life,
But hold to the same sharp-focussed ratio
Our blindness towards each other.

MYTHS

"Honestly, sir, what good are myths?"

(What good am I,
that is, whose myth is "sir."
One has to try:)

"Myths are the stuff that lives are made on . . ."

(No! Twenty faces guard their lives.
A girl who sleeps with swans. . . . What can you do
but lay eggs?
Or make it *real!*)

"Everybody likes to feel down?
Feel dawn?"

(Unsaid: "Oh perverse sir!")

"The Trojan War, a very important war . . ."

(But since the Bomb there are no wars no more,
only athletic contests. . . .

I'VE GOT IT, my mustardseed of faith:
I'll flap my hands and fly!

God! What a feat! Better than airplanes!
Floating here with my teaching finger out
like Gabriel!)

"This is the way it is! You're living a miracle!
Let's start a new world here!"

(But no again. They'd shoot me down, my hunters.
It says to in the handbook.)

"Mr. Jones, that was a very searching question.
Honesty is the best paucity."

THE RAPE OF EUROPA

After the painting by Titian in the Gardner Museum, Boston

He offered himself as game for women's hands
If they could lay to bulls that kind of straying
Idly beyond the reasonable fence and the square bull
    pasture
Towards the river side. He stopped their playing,
Made them fall back astonished by the sand
As, unforeseen, his gentleness alarmed.
Then, in fear of heightening their fear,
He paused and wonder danced alone in the air between.
His lung was quickened presently by a girl
Bolder than all the rest, sidling with laughter towards
    him.
But for the river she was all that moved,
A plait of flowers in her hand, desire in her limbs
For motion in the pattern of a dance
And the heaviness of strange intent about her.
Is there a heart not gathered by faint swaying,
This way, this way, accompanied by laughter?
Far within the circles of his body awakening
And moving at first outwards came the bull.
He tapped once, bowed his head and tapped again
As if to shake off springs of violence,
Then sank, for his great body was allayed
Partly and without malice he gazed there.
Soon the cowering girls made a ring about him;
Europa set her wreath upon his horns.
A silence fell that gave voice to the river
And the chapped rush of leaves. Then with a sigh,
As the Europa in each girl was loosed

9

To a corporeal rhythm, dance began.
Figures insinuated by desire
Flashed forth, evoking mushroom agonies
Or little wildernesses of turmoil
In the surprised beholder. Yet the dance
Trimmed their incipient fire to pattern still.
And the quiet music was answered by the bull
Only with breathing and abstracted eyes.
They were displeased by so much darkness garnered
Slothfully there and longed to see it rise.
Some struck him as they passed with whips of scarves
And some threw flowers. At last Europa dropped
Upon his back and stroked the glacial hide,
With her moist hands exploring pallid folds.
He could not bear the weight of that last garland
And all the impositions on his mood
By careless girls. He roused himself, therefore,
Out of the invisible chains of simple being
And joined them, moving faster as they moved
Until his foot was light with that sweet dancing.
But they are often slain who play with darkness
Or left behind near the original ground
Raising bruised fingers toward a blind ascension.
The bull, aflame, sprang for the water. Cries
Rebounded as if laughter struck blank walls
And the disheartened ring of virgins, flower
By its own beauty spoiled, fell back and broke.
Then they came together, as we see them here,
Trailing along the distant water's edge
Like the shucked petals of a ripened tale.

10

Clutching a horn, as her part taurine gown
Already mingles, chosen Europa rides.
The bull has leaped at once through sky and water
To harmonize with that which most dissolves;
He pulses toward fulfillment on a groundswell,
Followed by what the stewpots of the sea
Exhale: a fish flecked with the primal sunlight,
Runnels of foam. Love's bedfellows are here,
Planing the unforgettable blue in chubby disarray,
Their arrows bathed in Alpine clarity.
It is the seed-time of myth, strewing and passing over;
As in an hourglass when the sand drops free
The future spreads inexorably. Onward,
Where shafts of rock hoist the aspiring wave,
A couch is set; within an open meadow
A tentative cradle waxes in its tree.

THE COMBER

If Venus rose from the sea, then who am I?
For such a womb to stop at one
would be to nature's derogation—
and so I think we all rise from the sea,
separate and sisterly,
combing in the tidiness of fashion
here on the beach of time, and every
woman is a wave, a slower wave.

THE BOAR

Once there was a boar hunted by all.
Though some tempered spears and stayed at home
and others baked bread for those who went along,
staying at home themselves,
everybody in his heart was hunting.

The boar was never taken,
but ran in his wounds through the woods perpetually.
(I hear him running through those woods today,
grunting and goring.)

There are many ways to hunt: the bravest
get in among the still points of the spears,
that woods within a woods where the boar is
at the kill,

(though a kill never happens;
for what is the great body loping through
far glades of trees but the boar still?
There is at best only a resurrection
with all the bravest asleep round the new boar.)

The cowards make passes at the boar from afar
and write the poetry of hunting.

A few, it is said, turn from blood though pressed
even by their own blooded hearts' unrest,
and when the bakers bake, the slughorns blow,
they neither spin nor sow.

SPARROWS

Sparrows were lassoed by ironic eras,
Bundled with trees and breezes in the barn
Of sentimental stock. They're always with us,
Though, as the whole world to the palest stone
Is with us, moving out its life or death
Mysteriously beyond the equals sign.
How did they fly? Were holes a last resort,
A doubt left in the fabric of our barn?
For surely sparrows punctuate our lines
Again and breezes merit praise for blowing.

One can deny man's captions, not the thing
That they're attached to; little sparrows arched
Their bodies with a flair in hostile eras
And sallied through imaginary walls
Like scornful ghostlings. Even the bumptious air
Shatters our meaning with variety.
Blake had it, You must kiss them as they fly—
Or miss them. Lacking minds, perhaps, they live
Out there, companions in transience, live and thrive;
One that's denied will batten in your dreams.

VETERAN TIGER

The tiger is foliage and the foliage tiger.
If you strolled into him, you would, of course,
Find out what continent you were strolling in.
The tiger is foliage and the foliage tiger.

But camouflage is the tiger's pocket fortress,
More to ward off while he sleeps in the sun
Than to engage. At night his eyes burn forth;
But camouflage is the tiger's pocket fortress.

He thrives more by alchemy than vigor,
Pawing dead leaves to powder when they lie
Between him and his prey. Old tigers lose
Their vigor to the alchemy of pawing.

His final spring dispersed along lianas,
His body to the leaves, his growl to air,
The hunter finds dead tiger everywhere,
Dispersed along the longest of lianas.

GNU

The day I was eaten
began warmly under mother
as usual.
They called me a fool
to go from there to breakfast
unafraid.
My way's my way.

It was a decent calfhood,
the sleeping and eating part.
Before I had a chance at sex with gnus
a tiger deflowered me
by the throat.

Well, that's life
and this is afterlife
in the head of a man
who's playing with my name.
He has to look me up
in a book, of course,
to see if tigers really do it
to gnus.

I can't complain:
a little pleasure, a little fear,
one big event,
and then to have done with it.
In my will is my peace.

SONNET IN WINTER

Now stretch pale fibers of the day again
And the vast weaving that the sun betrays
Is lying open to the winter rain.
All color is an echoing of greys
Half danced to by the jagged evergreens.
The field's impassioned flowers have fought the sting
Of the cold long ago. A mandrake leans
In a locked swamp, the ice's overhang.
Shadows toward night grow till they loop the world.
The curved blade of their East cuts one by one
Dark patterns on the landscape. Soon the cold
Of light will tunnel through the air alone
And men will know how little can satisfy,
Watching a lonely star possess the sky.

YOUNG WOMAN IN FEVER

I am the animal inside my body,
the healthy and knowing squirrel
in a forest of malignancy.
When will the trees lower their mosses?
I want a clearing far from their ill sap!
Oh, if they hurt me
I can get smaller,
smaller than the fingers of their evil.
My name is Enid.

RIDDLE: THE SUCCESSFUL REALTOR

Herohood's out of reach
for the old indispensable octopus crying
"Bring me my telephones!"
But on the sly we love his virtues.

He's always at work among his neighborhoods
at the bottom of the sea,
which through his alien way become less strange.

He's always at work
and we, whose day must take
its underwater leap towards evening,
watch his joy.

It's like the joy of those we envy,
the lovers and pilgrims
and the train buffs
holding hands on the good excursion:
"Here we are in what we know so well!"

In the vacation of his character
he has all this without a journey.

Who is he?

TO ONE FOR WHOM POETRY AND MORALITY ARE INSEPARABLE

The skin of this peach is drawn
back in zigzags; in that
a baby Charybdis
of rot twists down
towards the peachstone
lazily. At 3',
5" the table bears
five oranges, one splitting
(like the peach), two pears and room
for more food.
                 Across the room
a girl, sexy, legs crossed,
intense as an animal,
has her skirt played with by
sunrays. On her finger
is a small diamond that recalls your mind.

THE NIGHT BEFORE THE
BAR MITZVAH

The used water pulls around his ankles
and backs off toward the hole
for what's not wanted in his world.
And he has come this far, dripping and clean,
an otter without wound.

Now the cold white sheets and the white night
printed for the last time with the Text,
its frayed edges glowing into color.

He chants his eighteen lines in a still tongue
and with the hypnotizing of his fear
sleep comes.

A GIRL

A girl who had fallen among Christians
tired of good Peter, good William, good Paul,
the Old Faithful of the Sunday social,
and sat above her long legs travelling
to Babylon.

But it was a little Babylon,
slow and remote,
and she had ripened too long on the wrong tree,
a fruit too dark now for the calm arrangement
of a pagan garden.

And so this ibis of a girl, this gift given
over and over to itself, returned
to the small town,
where each night when the stars shine,
from her childless room an answer
phosphoresces.

THE VACATION

No one to referee that game,
Poor fledglings, with their heads thrown back
And mastered hips joined to their shame,
Are lonely partners on the rack.

Who is that watchman of the night,
Stretched out, staring so vacantly
From his filled bed until the light
Of day permit activity?

And who lies breathing at his side,
In sleep a kind of ruffed grouse?
Is it the girl that neatly glides
About the duties of her house?

They married decent strangers; she
For images of his despair
Without her, for his good name; he
For guilt and the curling of her hair.

Yearly to interpose delight
They go upon their honeymoon
Again, where things are never quite
The same although they should be soon.

And a small cottage has sprung up
Near a favorite swimming cove;
Every summer they come up
To localize their straying love.

On starry nights after their meal
Old rituals of hand in hand
Begin and what they think they feel
Makes them lie upon cool sand.

So they tumble by that shore
Of the uncaring upland lake
As if it were not done before
And each moans for the other's sake.

AFTER IT

A fingertip, an earlobe, any hair
Led to the open country of love, my dear;
And we knew all the ports and all the countries.
But did we know our bodies'
Silent, peripheral, and other life
That pushes warts to light, withdraws them after
Like rock-faces in a primal sea?
It was that life, perhaps, gave you to me
Or me to you . . .
                    No matter:
Part of ourselves swam the same turbid water
And walked for a while the selfsame tropic land.
But as one forgets in time which arm was sprained,
Which finger cut, or which hand had the wart,
So we forgot the travelling lover's art
And stayed home in ourselves although together.

ON LEAVING THE ENGLISH LIBRARY

Reading the scholarly notes on vanished places,
Hebron and Babel, the mirror to lilacs,
And Athens, its stone piled upon old stone,
There danced antique young men about my mind
And girls whose hands caught by a sculptor's hand
Turned into flowers waved for a thousand years
That stranger girls could match them with their own.

And when the scholars wrote of soldier mummies
Like walnuts in their undecaying biers
With all their flails and arrows rusting near,
The imagination of my sex was stirred
By wasted concubines longing for princes,
Who decked themselves in veils and chaplets for
The delectation of a rival's eye.

Seeking the regent of the voiceless wood
At Versailles in the fall was reading too—
Another style of wandering down paths
Not scythed by my own hand. The king was hidden
Beyond the renewing green of his domain;
He caroused elsewhere with the Greek girls and boys,
The warriors and forgotten concubines.

Yet all danced in that absence, even stone:
Unlike the absence which avoids my text,
Hardly ferried across dividing waters
By note or snapshot. Now I must be one
Who goes at guilt-time home to a bare hearth
And a processional of empty rooms
Unfolded to the dying of my smile.

PARADE

The youngest son is riding on the plain;
Mother is ill, the last cow at the stalls:
"A week at most and seven dragons slain
To fill the niches of ancestral halls,"
He murmurs, counting merrily as he rides,
"And if some dragons fail to block my way,
Why then lost virgins will or lonely brides:
God, who makes youngest sons, will make the fray!"

Somehow, a land away, the roads are longer
And noble girls are chary of their sins.
Upon a brown mule, beggar-eyed with hunger,
Past rain-pocked statues of St. George, past inns
Whose rational keepers brook no free abiding,
The eldest son is riding, riding, riding.

DIAMONDS

Some men gradually begin seeing diamonds
as the world champions in staying power,
men of talent, men of sweetness,
who start off very well in the living kingdom.
What they don't have is
mind enough for choosing
between good and good.
And so their choices
erode their characters.
Before they grow too weak in the flowering,
dying human world, they make
one last hard choice
to put their faith in diamonds.
Then all the decisions are made forever
by Talmudic Jews in Amsterdam
with telescoping monocles
and chisels like the Lord's on Sinai.

FROM CAESAR'S CAMP:
A POLITICAL FANTASY

"Only the supple inherit the people" OLD SAYING

FIRST OFFICER

"He appears in strange territories boldly
And eyes the bulging tribute pouches coldly,
Our young snake of an imperator, Max.
First, the recusant pagans to the ax
('We're all Romans here. We know what's what!'),
Then a Forum, a Colosseum and all that.
But all that civilization's after us:
We're at the brunt of things with Max the Glorious!"

SECOND OFFICER

"Freedom lies over the edge of expectation.
Caesar is free. Such dark paths he can choose from!
With their brains dimly glowing to prevent falls,
Most people daily waddle where the flesh calls.
Caesar, like inexorable bone,
The grim geometry of the skeleton,
Underlies things. His will cuts scruple like a razor.
Others obey the law of not being Caesar."

THIRD OFFICER

"He alone is pointed to by the past.
Old men who remember oldtime Caesars nest
Trembling among friends or thumb the archives
While stranger bees invade the golden hives.
And after, when the farms darken, who dares
Suggest the grain be sifted from the tares?
Old wisdom is not wanted; one is wise
To make a sheath of words for Caesar's policies."

SECOND OFFICER

"Like an idea Caesar is everywhere
And men, as rational animals, think it; here
On the northern border and in the desert town
Or bedded with their virgin wives at Rome.
He's master of each village, seen, unseen,
And trees for thousands of miles over the horizon.
No matter what he does, all buildings remain
Sunning within his empire, from India to Spain."

FIRST OFFICER

"Contradictions, if bold, prove him to us
Like victories. We move to the subtle choice
Of countermarch as to attack. And rout
Itself is but the heavens reaching out
To touch him like an oak in a thunderstorm.
Of course, too many defeats and the hoods come
With their unanswerable knives and thongs,
But Max rations defeat as garnish for our songs."

THIRD OFFICER

"He will be stabbed someday by a retainer,
One of the scarred kind, an old soldier
And family man, upon whose arm he rested
His own in foul times, one whose love he wasted,
Being careless to inflict the private grief
Which cuts through love an opening for the knife."

CRUMBGIVING

Only from our point of view, as masters of the table,
does the eater of crumbs glow with a terrible
        loveliness.
He clings to our pity like a bat,
certainly. And a few, independent of the prince,
think that disgusting,
our table his rafter.
They miss the light in his face when we bowl him
        the crumb.
For a moment he sees it with the fullest glance, a baby's,
his crumb without compare.
There is nothing else in the world but its hollows,
        its rims,
bounding dreamily over the tablecloth like sagebrush.
From a distance he drinks the shadows in, facet by facet,
and swells.
What a pleasure to hear us, the masters, counting—
        two, ah,
three
until, lovingly, it's his!

POLLS

A secret I know about China,
huge and twitching land of rumor
and cloud mountain, goes:
After a thousand years of news
from the press invented there
and speeches for that press, the polls
as slow and sure as quicksand
drank all history down
and left only story, like the villain's hat,
afloat on the foam.

FROM THE GRAYBOOK

Work at making less to touch
of yourself and of things.
More against nakedness than anyone,
live in skins up to the nostril
held open still for breathing.

Very little happens on horizons you watch,
though sometimes in a corner the newborn
scapegoat gets to suck or suck twice.
When you hear of it,
sense the old stakeout in your body—
everything new wants to nest in you—
and pave everywhere to keep the life down.

AN URBAN CHRISTMAS

So many wreaths and trees are hostages
For the withdrawing spirit. Even the jails
Are covered with them and the station houses
Twinkle in boughs and bulbs a festive welcome.
Where are the children merciful enough
To say they believe in Santa still? I watched
His vicar shot at by a ten-year-old
Armed with a toy ballistic missile launcher.
I laughed, of course—one cannot choose but laugh
And ride the loaded escalator down.

So many old distractions are at hand
To grace the time. Widows beguile the lunch hour
By decorating ledges on the airshaft
And in the park mild, city-loving deer
Are fed popcorn by priests.
                            Silence surrounds
All the pieties of this gone world
Laid out in spangles under a cold sky.
The city bears its unconnected sorrows,
From furnished rooms where egg nog watchers sleep,
Old men shepherding their loneliness,
To houses of the merry gentlefolk
Before which coeds sing of Bethlehem.

FROM HERE TO THERE

Here is the highway of dead birds,
the hopeless dodging animals. Skunkbloom,
that is the last defense, the finest;
a small broken body is the other,
though sometimes it's unholy length of dog
dead sideways two three four,
the legs in the air the horror.

And this is the highway of from here to there,
route such and such intestate,
clean for the most part, nothing in between
except the foursquare talking in the car
and the foursquare watching silence, covered over
by the car's baked metal skin.

And so we have two worlds, one out, one in,
dying to cross each other.

3 A.M.

The hospital rises in a foursquare void;
North, east, west, south, the flowers are down,
Varieties of afternoon birds flown;
If bats litter the sky, the sky is a bat,
The hospital glowing brokenly through its wings.

Elsewhere is breathing and the darker functions
Valve and unvalve in darkness and the sea moves
Sowing its clams under the world's foreskin;
Shells prey upon shells and empty them—
But that is backhanded life and of the void.

Yes, other stone remains in the watchman's hand
And though the restaurants have given up,
Leaving their Maginot Line of chairs to the night,
The sun will waken on a brickwork shoulder.
For the eye of dawn things will spread out,
Tower and flower, whatever is in hiding,
The watchman lose the familiar room again,
His table, chair, and lunchpail to the light—
He will lose the burden of keeping it all together.

Now we are wires between abundant charges,
From sun to sun: the nurse who plots the line
Declining on the fever chart towards morning,
While she patrols her corridor of wounds,
The watchman, and the watcher . . . If we snap?

Far away on Blue Hill, above twigs and brambles
And quiet pressed lairs,
Rises the cleft observatory, the knife in its heart—
All night the exposure festers forth new stars.

36

THESE DAYS

for James Lewisohn

These days the sunlight almost seems total.
A few men, trees, stand between heaven and earth.
In the light of their shadows we others are
    reading, still,
messages the dead have stopped sending,
these days of almost fatal sunlight.

SONNET

As suburbs are the rings of hearkening
To the great city's cry, so is this hood
That has been thrown about me, although rude,
Yet the impatient caping of my spring.
I cannot tell what the ripe year will bring
When it flees haunted on before these crude
First sessions of despair, nor what the lewd
And ghost-tainted brain will learn to sing.
But if by nightly forays in the world
Of pictures that a childhood stored away,
By charting the transparent lands that lie
Between the cedar trees, one thought is whirled
Into an action that outlasts its day,
My shadow wears the stone it passes by.

THE HAWK

Before this hour is pried by the hawk's wing
Rising from its grey nest above the lawns
And shades of the lifting day, early to fling
A furrow in the sun and cleave our songs
Apart from the strong and heartless not our own,
I would hurl nets of cries into the air
To wind the hawk in flight that he drop down,
Himself prey to this questioning, this fear:
"Before the roofs fly from our shallow hells
And there is green fire that unties the pen
With flowering of the flesh in syllables
To pilfer each thing from its foxes den,
O hawk, we must make whole what you have torn—
What womb must we sleep in to be reborn?"

AN AUTUMN POEM

The rain, oscilloscoping, heels the roses
Clinging like suicides to the stalk, but most
Have fallen petalwise to dissolution.
Through the stripped maples ads deceive again
And streetcars roll. The garden is shrinking now
Into the piecemeal absence cold requires,
With canvas over the fountains and the birdbath.
Winter is a drugged suitcase in my attic
And a leap in time. Soon mantles will be shaken,
All gardens lie in pantherskins of snow
And six more weeks be gone. Small things lose force;
The grass itself flags in the general dying.
I'd not be stung by honeybees here, posting
Shock from head to toe again and again.

It is the tawny season
When enviable climates warm the mind—
Blue skullcaps over the twofold Thebaid.
In Greece "come, come into the desert" sang
The sainted birds who catered to the spring
Of Laius, and in Egypt holy men
Ignored the foliage of metropolis.

What were they seeking on the thirsty margin
Of fire? Was it forty days as one
For a good look at God? I am sick with time
And shrink within this bandage of a room
From where innumerable changing gardens stretch
To the desert sun. Navel of my desire:
The windowpane's smug water exiles me
From the dissolving seasons and the dry.

40

THE MOLE

A Poem for Camp Counselors

When darkness had snubbed to sleep even Bruce the
     Wild,
I oiled my face and hands against night life
And went outside. In the wet air stars shone
Like flies wiping their forelegs. It was pleasant
To patrol slowly through hemlocks rising from sand
Here and there in the catlike stillness. Chaired,
Afterwards, in great roots above the ground,
I read Jane Austen with a flashlight pen.
But long, feminine mosquitoes coming in
To my English estate in the Maine woods
Made me break off.
                A whippoorwill slung volleys
From the back brush as I walked the next patrol.
I wanted human trespass, though; jailed gardens,
Fireside cats and dogs, the city . . .
I foraged beyond my itching summer body
When the eelgrass near my shoe gave him away.

The mole was young, but huffed as he climbed over
His mound; and it was there that I caught him,
Closing the neutral box of my hands around—

Then my hands, turning human, closed around me.

ALL'S WELL AT THE HOTEL

The slightly deformed waitress in black rayon
And white cuffs wanted me or the Arab page,
Melmel. Our fantail boss, doling the pay on
Thursdays, remembered when he was my age
And worked for less. All's well at the hotel
Still, I'm sure. The Methodist minister
Rents room and radio for the double-header
On Sunday afternoons. As when Eve fell
The snake slid down the tree, our elevator
Pimp descends counting from an upper floor.
I have escaped them; all's well that ends well.

Yet, sometimes, I catch myself in looking back
To that sad hive, to the Arab, to the boss squawking
At Jean, our waitress . . .

                      I've seen her in the park
Where V's widen as paved walks meant for walking.

THE WRESTLERS

Yesterday, after twenty years
Schools, businesses, and wars,
I met my wrestling partner Bert
B. He was the boy who taught
The nelson, half and full, to the grammar school.
But Bert was no fool;
He kept tricks in his bag. I tried,
And when "Uncle" was cried for, I cried,
Holding out longer if girls were there.
He is a bull now. I am a bear;
Neither wants to talk for long—
But, yesterday, in a glance it seemed
Our little lost bodies sprang
Toward sweat and the mat again.

MY CROWNS

for Dr. Pontifex

That was wings too,
like everything not rigid,
everything between two
people or a people and its city
or a cloud and its sky.

The dentist and I
worked my teeth for half a year,
the New Boston rising from its pad
outside our window.
And as he drilled deeper
the development reached higher
and I grew older
until all was capped with gold:
his fee, the sky,
the stumps that lined my jaw,
that aching row.

I am complete now
though the city is still changing.
I miss the man
whose intelligence
lay wholly in his competence,
all clouded beside.
Such friendships end
when the skill that called them up has run
its course.

Everything human has wings
(better to name it that than decay)
and flies toward an inevitable future:
a city, a body, warmth between two men;
everything has its day—except,
of course, my golden crowns.

THE WORD

From a chamber behind my eyes drops the word
    "Treasure",
born of irony out of longing,
a word without friends in a Spartan world.
It lies here, outshining the erasable
bond, the yellow obstetric pencil.
I have the heart to kill it
and say, "Aw c'mon, word, die!
Go back, *il mio tesoro*, if you can't die,
to the literature that owns you."

But I know how it is, even on this page, with babies—
one wordless day
I'll find myself becoming grateful.

WALL

Out of the strummed nerves of getting by
I come to where the wall is.
Squirrels tunnel against it under the ivy.
I know where the bricks are without winter to show me.
The sky, too thin for nerves, too simple to be a man,
spreads over it;
but everything I call the world stops here.

Back in my life, when objects failed, I moved them
like a young chessplayer winning through
to the bright outside of fame
by moving his old furniture about.
Here the wall is,
old, and new—immoveable.

Another world, mysterious wood or holy city,
stretches its fingertips of tower and twig
on the far side.
Men and women who walk through stone have
        reached it.
Can I?

If so, I would have the wall still rising behind me
like the sober heart of a story that ends well.
There is enough left in me of the good Jew
to need a wall somewhere to come back to.

IN MEMORY OF MY FATHER

The Newspaper
A strange seduction.
I find myself a young man
in my father's habit,
his old browsing eternity
with the news.

All of it feeds me—
the sports and the comics,
the front page with its many graves,
editorials,
horse-blinders and loss.

When we were in this life together
I read like an educated man.

ii
Where it clearly stops
Almost a child again, grown from wading,
I walk past the end of your life
where it clearly stops.

iii

The Steel Ball

The best of what they say means
"You've got the steel ball
that we had."
Hardly a word more that's right,
as if to describe
something so round
and so around
were impossible.

I've got the aching steel ball.
Oh I've got it
to come on or be come on by
each day while it grows small.

Keeping faith,
I approach the ball as a kind of life
whose feeling I now hold
in trust, waiting somehow.

Where is eternity? I am looking.

THE HORN WAITS

In a room I was getting used to
I found in dust beneath the couch
a microscopic hunting horn
I lost as a child.
(It is my luck to find the things I need
exiled from where I lost them.)
Dust, gentle dust,
coated from my eyes the horn rungs
and stopped, an ageing hill, the mouth of the horn.

I reached down, but my fingers would not take it
as they sloped like pagodas over it.
My eyes began to blur.
And now the couch is back, corner on corner.

Inviolable dust,
there seemed, as always in your little worlds,
a chance to set out again through deserts.

TRAINING THE EYE

for Oscar Sanborn of Weld

It seems the corridors of my childhood
live behind me and shrink as living people:
the one at grammar school I stumbled down
alone during classhour, sick to my stomach,
it was a kind of endless Karnak
as I wound my arms around a pillar
and said, "I will remember this forever,"
noting within my nausea.

It's there, unfairly small,
as our assembly hall is there
with its picture, "The British Burning Buffalo."
Each of the colors is an orphan
now that I've grown, seen Turner and Renoir.

But can all this be so
in the gradual world of villages?
Few leave to be surprised at a dog's growth
on their return, or a field of trees—
the sadness of losing out from watching.
And death diminishes like the road from town.

THE FEAR OF LIGHTNING

With many hills around us and tall trees
nearer to the rain, we always
feel our nakedness is special.

Somewhere my name is on a death,
but whether it sits sunning among fruit
and fruit decay
or canters like a nightmare behind me,
I hardly know.

And the best that I can do
is always to feel death as an ambience,
caring, but not hurrying my feet
though the warrant-laden sky
should, like a parent, find me.

MY ROAD,

because there is always craft
I have not looked you in the face.

What am I to do with
what I cannot understand,
the ground and the brook and the tears in my eyes?
Not to have been born
is the best friend
of the pure particular places.

My hand's as good as any toad;
the different flashes of my clothes
go with the grass—
something to touch is not the bigot.
What am I to do with
what I distill,
an anger in the breathing?
How can I narrow further to the saying?

When I'm working I see the grass most clearly,
the orange alder root at home
in tough bourgeois
possession of the soil,
and, after nights of rain,
gentle mud laminating the ditches.

THE ELEMENTS

The elements I have by heart
are stone and water.
Happy the poets with all four!

I buy and grow
and sleep with my collection,
take inventory too:

And then, for any day,
a bug climbing a brick is,
with the right hold of my mind,
Sinon climbing the walls of Troy
or the hero, on all fours, over
the pit in Haggard's *She*.

I am afraid to see my life this way,
though every year
like Actaeon I mislay the fear
at times out of time
that strangely devour and leave one.

The bug goes on with his instinct
over the brick the seasons wear,
with hours enough to get a life in.

LONG PULL

I am here
rowing backward from my poems
and the poems of others.
Goodbye. How could I stay
at the dock of their homecoming?
I row from summer
with its flickers and cold stoves
on the long pull.

Behind me the abyss
thunders around its parched
coinspace of an eye.
Perhaps the coin is stamped
with a first noun.

I will row home
when the shore is strange enough.

Henry Braun was born in Olean, New York in 1930 and grew up in Buffalo. He received his B.A. in French Literature from Brandeis University, spent a year in France on a Fulbright Scholarship, and returned to Brandeis for his M.A. He then spent several years in Boston as a social worker and a museum guide. He has taught at Boston University and at the University of Maine. At present he is Assistant Professor of English at Temple University in Philadelphia, where he lives with his wife, Joan, and their two daughters. During the summer, he and his family live on an isolated farm in the mountains of northwestern Maine.